WONDERFUL NATURAL WONDERS

THE EVERGLADES

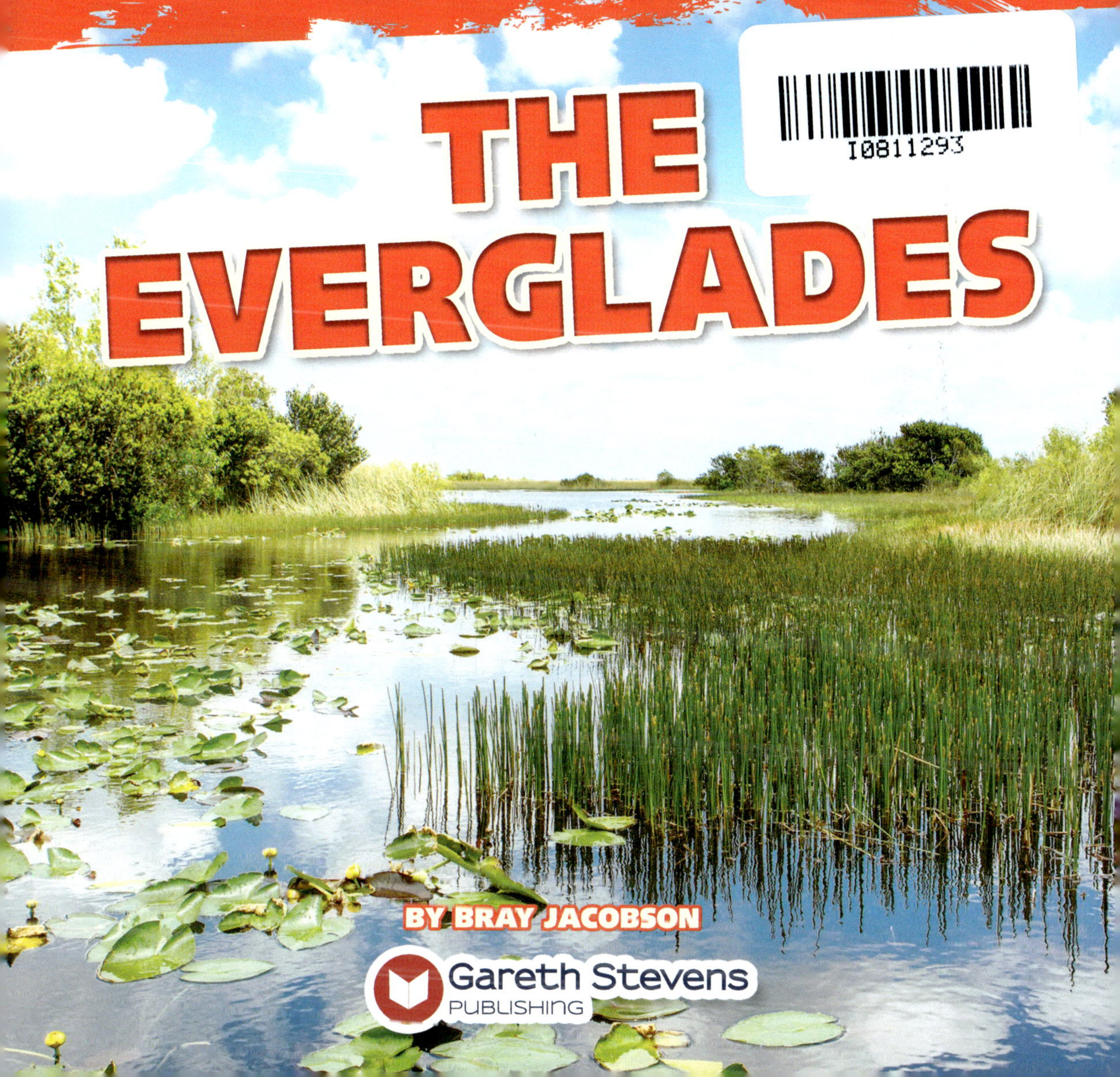

BY BRAY JACOBSON

Gareth Stevens PUBLISHING

Please visit our website, www.garethstevens.com. For a free color catalog of all our high-quality books, call toll free 1-800-542-2595 or fax 1-877-542-2596.

Library of Congress Cataloging-in-Publication Data
Names: Jacobson, Bray, author.
Title: The Everglades / Bray Jacobson.
Description: New York : Gareth Stevens Publishing, [2023] | Series: Wonderful natural wonders | Includes index.
Identifiers: LCCN 2021036692 (print) | LCCN 2021036693 (ebook) | ISBN 9781538276747 (set) | ISBN 9781538276754 (library binding) | ISBN 9781538276730 (paperback) | ISBN 9781538276761 (ebook)
Subjects: LCSH: Natural history–Florida–Everglades–Juvenile literature. | Wetland ecology–Florida–Everglades–Juvenile literature. | Everglades (Fla.)–Environmental conditions–Juvenile literature.
Classification: LCC QH105.F6 J34 2023 (print) | LCC QH105.F6 (ebook) | DDC 578.76809759/39–dc23
LC record available at https://lccn.loc.gov/2021036692
LC ebook record available at https://lccn.loc.gov/2021036693

Published in 2023 by
Gareth Stevens Publishing
29 E. 21st Street
New York, NY 10010

Designer: Tanya Dellaccio
Editor: Kristen Nelson

Photo credits: Cover Irina Wilhauk/Shutterstock.com; background texture (pp 3-24) BEMPhoto_31/Shutterstock.com; p. 5 FloridaStock/Shutterstock.com; p. 7 (background) arigato/Shutterstock.com; p. 7 (map) BigMouse/Shutterstock.com; p. 9 Galyna Andrushko/Shutterstock.com; p. 11 Liga Cerina/Shutterstock.com; p. 13 jo Crebbin/Shutterstock.com; p. 15 Grahof/Shutterstock.com; p. 17 Nick Fox/Shutterstock.com; p. 19 Heiko Kiera/Shutterstock.com; p. 21 Mia2you/Shutterstock.com.

Printed in the United States of America

CPSIA compliance information: Batch #CSGS23: For further information contact Gareth Stevens, New York, New York at 1-800-542-2595.

CONTENTS

Boldface words appear in the glossary.

Special Ecosystem

The Everglades **ecosystem** is unlike any other. Its name puts together the words "glade" and "ever." A glade is a grassy area in a forest or **swamp**. "Ever" likely has to do with how large this area is. It's truly a natural wonder.

Wetland

The Everglades ecosystem is found in southern Florida. It's a **wetland** more than 4,300 square miles (11,100 sq km) in size. Almost all the land of the Everglades is covered in water during the wet season, from about May to October.

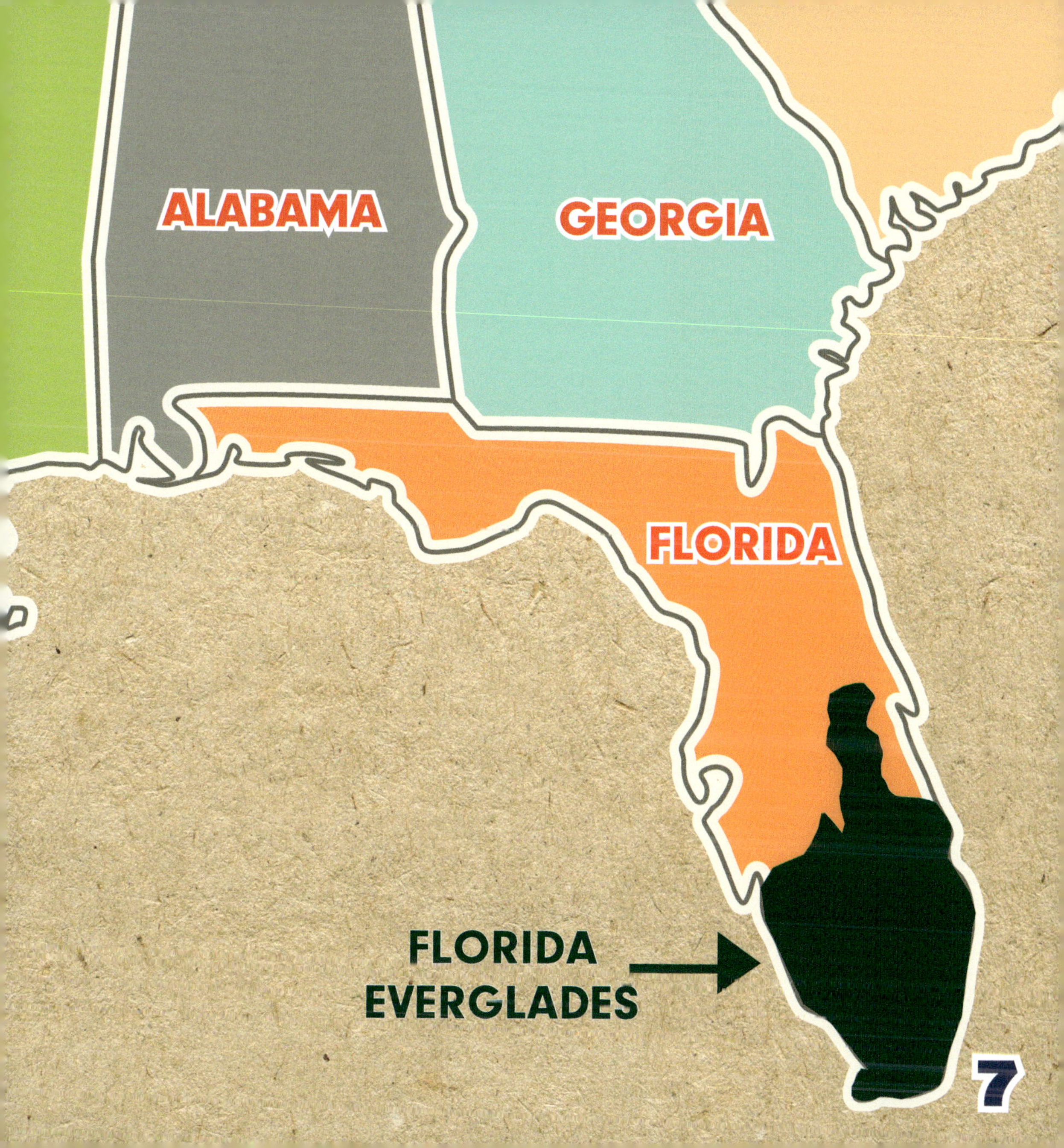
ALABAMA
GEORGIA
FLORIDA
FLORIDA
EVERGLADES

The water flows slowly south through the grasses of the Everglades. It's called the "river of grass." It reaches the Gulf of Mexico and Florida Bay. It moves through many different kinds of **habitats**. These include swamps featuring trees like cypresses and mangroves.

CYPRESS TREES

Important for People

The Everglades ecosystem is important to the people living near it. It makes the water **quality** better. About a third of people living in Florida get their drinking water from it. A lot of Florida's farmland gets water from the Everglades too.

Plants and Animals

From ponds to forests, the habitats of the Everglades are home to many kinds of plants and animals. Saw grass is widespread. Water lilies commonly grow on top of the water. The Everglades is home to the Florida panther, crocodile, and manatee, among many others.

WATER LILIES

The plants and animals of the Everglades need the water levels of the ecosystem to change over the year. A certain amount of water is needed for some animals to **breed**. The white ibis, wood stork, and many herons all breed in the Everglades.

WHITE IBIS

Everglades at Risk

For a long time, people living near the Everglades harmed it. They **diverted** water. They changed the ecosystem by building cities and farmland. Finally, the U.S. government decided to **protect** the Everglades ecosystem. The southernmost part became Everglades National Park in 1934.

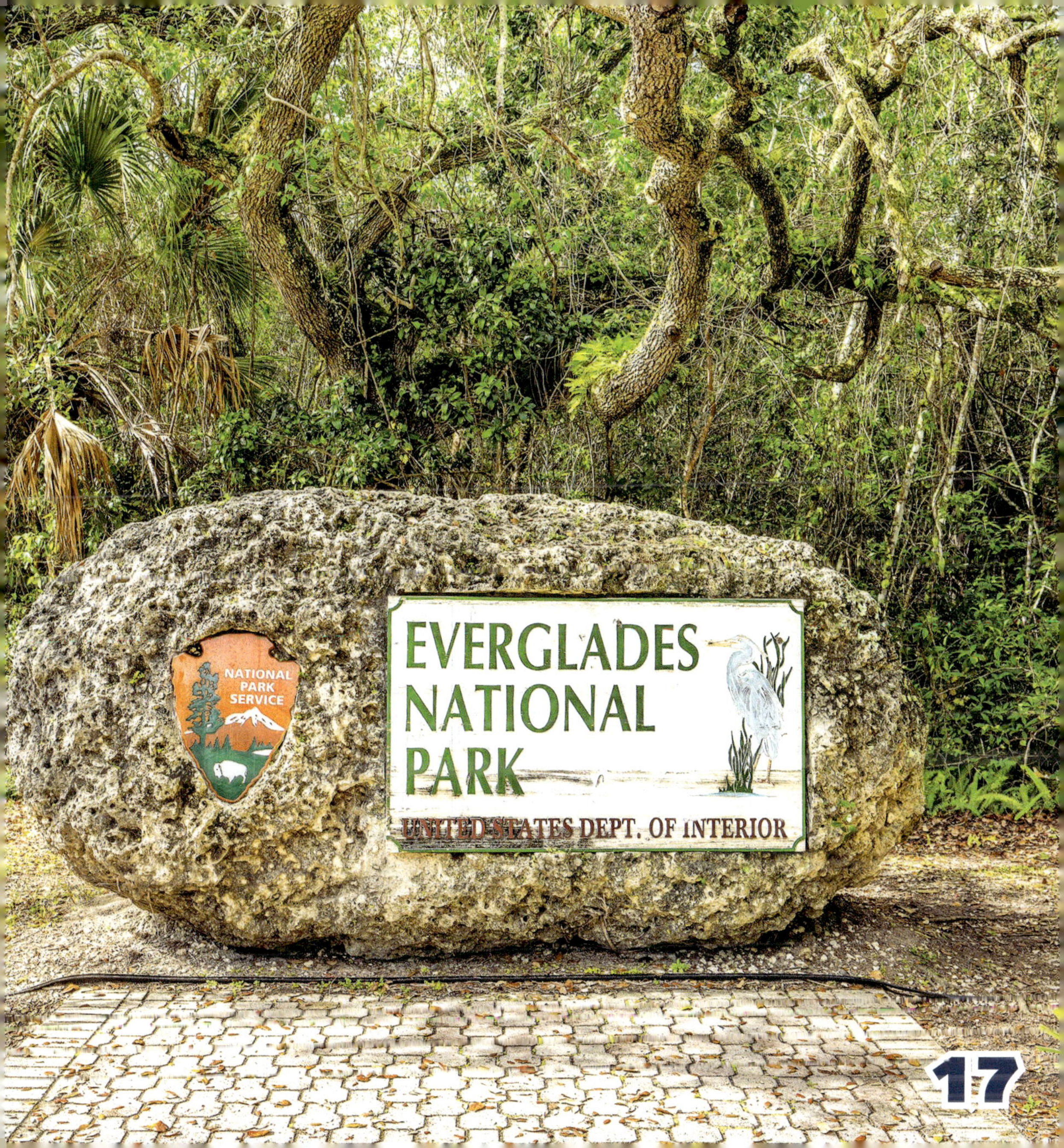
NATIONAL PARK SERVICE
EVERGLADES NATIONAL PARK
UNITED STATES DEPT. OF INTERIOR

Today, the Everglades still needs help. **Invasive species**, such as the Burmese python, harm native plants and animals. Cities have continued to grow, shrinking the Everglades ecosystem. Water is stopped from flowing the way it should. **Conservation** of the Everglades is an ongoing effort.

BURMESE PYTHON

National Park

As many as a million people visit Everglades National Park each year. There, they see the beauty that needs to be protected. They can also bike or canoe around the park. Many visitors fish or camp in the wonder that is the Everglades!

GLOSSARY

breed: to come together to produce babies

conservation: care for the natural world

divert: to change the path taken by something

ecosystem: all the living things in an area

habitat: the natural place where a plant or animal lives

invasive species: one kind of living thing likely to spread and be harmful when in a new area

protect: to keep safe

quality: the standard or grade of something

swamp: an area with trees that is covered with water at least part of the time

wetland: land containing high levels of moisture in the soil and usually covered with water at least part of the time

FOR MORE INFORMATION

BOOKS

Minsky, Howie. *In the Everglades*. Ann Arbor, MI: Cherry Lake Publishing, 2020.

Nelson, Penelope S. *Everglades National Park*. Minneapolis, MN: Jump!, 2020.

WEBSITES

Everglades National Park
kids.nationalgeographic.com/nature/article/everglades
Read more about the Everglades on the National Geographic for Kids website.

Everglades National Park
www.nps.gov/ever/index.htm
Find out more about visiting Everglades National Park on the National Park Service's website.

Publisher's note to educators and parents: Our editors have carefully reviewed these websites to ensure that they are suitable for students. Many websites change frequently, however, and we cannot guarantee that a site's future contents will continue to meet our high standards of quality and educational value. Be advised that students should be closely supervised whenever they access the Internet.

INDEX